Don't Tell the Cat...

GRAZIA VALCI

Don't Tell the Cat...

How to Take Care of Your Cat Without... Turning Him into a Tiger!

English Translation by Anne Milano Appel

GREMESE

Drawings: Yolanda Zerboni

Original title: Non lo dire al Gatto...

Translation revised by: Shula Atil Curto

Cover: Studio associato Pardini, Apostoli, Maggi – Rome

Phototypeset:
Graphic Art 6 s.r.l. – Rome

Printed and bound by:
BEFORE s.r.l. – San Benedetto del Tronto

Copyright GREMESE
2001 © E.G.E. s.r.l. – Rome

All rights reserved. No part of this book
may be reproduced, recorded or transmitted
in any way or by any means without the prior
consent of the Publisher.

ISBN 88-7301-467-4

Introduction

Shhh... don't tell the Cat.... It's a piece of advice which Humans whisper to one another in almost all families where His Majesty, the Cat, lives when they don't want to make him aware of something which might alarm him or arouse his protests: like a visit to the vet, for example. Yet – let there be no mistake about it – the idea of lowering one's voice turns out to be a useless precaution with a creature like our four-footed friend who is anything but stupid or naive.

Generally speaking, in fact, even if a Human speaks very slowly – being overly prudent and choosing a word whose meaning might be difficult even for many of us – Pretty-Tail, the sly one, while perhaps even pretending not to listen, will immediately get the message. Sounds which our ear would never be aware of hardly ever escape his extremely sensitive hearing, so it is useless to speak in a whisper to avoid being overheard by him. Not only that, but he even understands from our actions when he is being talked about and what is being said about him. He undoubtedly understands that he is the center of the discussion, not only by the meaning of a given word or the intonation of a phrase, but by a certain furtiveness or over-cautiousness on our part which leads us to broadcast our intentions by glancing in his direction. And should you be surprised by this and voice your astonishment out loud, you will see a flash of amusement and even – why not? – ironic sympathy in the beautiful, iridescent pupils of Mimi, Felix, Paco, Fur Ball, Arthur, Sugar and company. To exchange a look of understanding with our Pretty-Tail, who generally grants us his affectionate complicity, is one of the most touching moments of our life together; but the cost of trying to betray him or underestimate him can instead be a slight – but alas oh so stinging – wound to our pride. And yes, on certain occasions we have to understand the degree to which our superiority as Humans can turn into presumptuousness. It's as simple as that.

Therefore, rather than not informing the Cat of intentions that concern him, or trying not to be overheard by him when we discuss them with other Humans, we should ask ourselves how we can communicate these plans to him without making him angry.

The controversial expedience of big words

Try a little experiment: this too won't fail to amaze you. Pronounce an unusual word which he, your four-footed friend, has never heard, and you will discover that that alleged human supremacy we were talking about will never succeed in bringing him down. In short, we invite you to play a kind of game with your Cat, along the lines of a television quiz or game show, the kind where the contestants are fed a string of infrequently used words of dubious meaning, in order to test their preparation, intuition or ability to reason (and to shell out lovely sums of money to them, should they succeed in guessing). So then, observe your feline friend while you say to him, I don't know? Nebuchanezzar. From the loftiness of your cultural background, you will think to yourselves: "He really doesn't know that the great Babylonian king, whose

name was in fact Nebukadrezzar (later distorted in the Bible into the version we know, and which Giuseppe Verdi set to music) had it in for the Egyptians, let's be honest. This would be a reason why he should hate him, given the fact that he's a Cat and his ancestors were very much loved by those people. He would howl his meows to the heavens, if he only knew". And instead? Our friend, instead, will widen his big eyes, and prick up his ears and vibrissas; he will hunch over as though collecting his thoughts in meditation. In the pupils – green, azure, golden – you will certainly read bewilderment at first, but then their fixity and a change in color to intense black in a yellow circle will give you a clue to the attention His Majesty is devoting to the enigma. Don't be surprised if it appears that he has gotten to the bottom of the mystery (though without really grasping the literal meaning) and reached a decision as to whether it's worth his further attention or not. Agreed, he will not know exactly what you mean – but what the heck! You're asking too much from a Cat who hasn't been to school like you have. Yet you are exactly right in thinking that the importance of the experiment, at least, has not escaped him. Not only that, but he has stored the name away in a kind of file of things he knows, which every living creature maintains in his brain. He has also tagged it with one of the many labels at his disposal: "to be saved", "to be forgotten", "to be feared", "don't give it any importance" and so on. In short, it's as if your Cat knew the meaning of names, as if he knew the individuals and the objects, and is like a small repository of knowledge.

We suspect, therefore, that in addition to the fact that concepts do not escape him, even the nuances of our discussions hold no secrets from him. We wonder, for example, if he is not aware of certain old adages which have it in for Cats. And we wonder how he manages not to harbor hard feelings against them for the gratuitous cruelty, the mean spirit, and above all the ignorance (so much ignorance!) which they express.

Don't tell the Human

I will enjoy your amazement when you read this codicil of mine, the first of several that I will sow here and there among the author's annotations. Not to show off my learning and culture. That's all we need! And without any pretense of instructing the ignorant. Ignorant, that is, in the sense that there's something they don't know about their knowledge. Far be it from me to offend anyone, for one thing because I believe that by inserting my comments, we'll attract more readers. Comments or commentaries? I like the second term better. Meanwhile Humans are ignorant of the fact that we Cats know how to read their writing. Otherwise what good would years and years of practice be – years of sitting on their books, on the pages of their newspapers, on the sheets of their notepads? Have they never asked themselves if our observation of their typewriters, at first, and later of their computer keyboards was really mere curiosity

rather than an in-depth and comparative study of how certain of their devices work? By now we know how to use the various keyboards. As for the mouse, we still have some difficulty with it. Above all because we can't resist the temptation to throw it down and chase it into every corner of the house, wherever it may go and hide. It's not called a mouse for nothing. And by

the way, the decision to call it a mouse, a useless animal, if ever there was one, when the computer's breed is actually quite a useful object has not gone down well at all with us Cats. It's another instance of the inconsistency of their behavior: with real mice they act ridiculously, shouting, jumping up on chairs, almost as though they were afraid of an insignificant creature with four flimsy little paws whom we Cats can wipe out with a single blow. So then why call it a mouse and not a cat?

Speaking just to myself, I am pleased by the fact that she has not spoken of Human "masters" but only of alleged human superiority. Alleged, mind you. In fact, we Cats do not have masters. On the contrary. Often and gladly, as they say, it is we ourselves who boss them around in their homes, and it seems that our behavior, which they call putting on airs, frequently puts them in awe of us. As for that...

He must be given a name

According to many ethologists, it is not only advisable but downright essential to give the Cat a name as soon as he enters the home, whether he is adopted, purchased or rescued from the street, whether he is acquired in what Gabriele D'Annunzio called "feline infancy" or is already an adult. It seems the name is important to make him understand human authority. Granting for the sake of argument that he is willing to accept that authority. Which is almost always the case, for one thing because our four-footed friend, whatever you may say about him, is neither ungrateful nor disloyal, and very much appreciates the person who gives him care and affection. Saying his name gently or harshly serves to make the feline aware of our satisfaction or disapproval.

In his name he will recognize the mark of his human friend; the name will be a reminder and a certainty for him: in short, a point of reference.

Notwithstanding the title of this handbook, we feel that it is useful to say to the Feline, without any hesitation: "Do you like this name? Is it okay with you, or would you prefer being called something different?". If nothing else, it will serve to fix the name in his mind. In fact, as soon as the name is selected, it is worth repeating it like a prolonged call until he gets used to it. Yet our four-footed friend will never be able to let us know whether he likes the name or not: whether he finds it appropriate, attractive or unsuitable. All the same, you should not select a name which is ugly, ridiculous or offensive, thinking that it won't matter since the quadruped cannot rebel: keep in mind that sooner or later neighbors, friends and acquaintances will hear you calling your Cat's name. What impression will you make as you repeat "Emmenthal, Rigoletto, Wise-Guy" and other similar pleasantries? Even if your Pretty-Tail doesn't know that his name has made him seem ridiculous, it goes without saying that you and only you will be the one to lose face in the end. Angelo Lombardi, an ethologist who won notoriety for having introduced animals to television in the Fifties, wrote: "Among all the domesticated animals... cats are the ones with whom we have the most complicated and delicate relationship... If we wanted to add to the paradox, we could say that although the dog is man's friend, it is man who is the cat's friend... Even the most common, most disadvantaged, most wretched cat shares an undeniable intelligence with his human companions...". Why then humiliate our gentle friend?

On the contrary, the majority of Cat owners – pardon me, Cat friends – let themselves get carried away by their imagination when they pet their cats or call them. Agreed, the house Cat has a name and must have one: whether selected by chance, by pure coincidence, or agreed upon after more or less lengthy debates among family members. And if he is noble and comes from an illustrious lineage – read pedigree – it should be a name chosen to make a fine impression upon the crest or pedigree, whichever you wish to call it. Yet in daily life, Humans end up addressing their feline master with the strangest, most affectionate terms of endearment. The beauty of it is that he responds knowing very well that he is the object of those expressions, even the most unusual ones: "mama's little darling, Itsy-Bitsy, sweetie-pie...". For convenience, in this handbook, we too have referred to His Majesty by various appellations ranging from four-footed friend to Pretty-Tail, to the simplest of all, "He".

The inspiration for these notes is a beautiful Pussy Meow, whose name is almost onomatopoeic. To tell the truth, his behavior is not exemplary; it should be explained that animals, like Humans, also have different personalities and characters, and therefore their attitudes and reactions vary. But many experiences in the life of a feline repeat themselves, and comparing them can help us understand many subtleties in the world of the Cat. For example, among Pussy Meow's traits is that of turning a deaf ear when he hears the usual call – "here pussy pussy" – to which all his fellow cats respond. But no, this Pussy Meow is accustomed to coming when you whistle, just as if he were a dog. We don't know if he does it to distinguish himself, or because he may have lived with a dog in early kittenhood. He was already about six months old when we took him into our home. Another Pussy Meow, on the other hand (related to the first only by the color of his coat: a very lovely ginger tabby), not only doesn't like being called, since he and he alone decides when to appear, but even gets to the point of squaring off, like a boxer, standing solidly on his hind paws – kangaroo style – when he feels there is an excessive, annoying insistence. He also fights when he hears words that sound threatening to him.

Names for them, the Humans

All right: we're the Quadruped, the Feline, the Pussycat, or more pompously His Majesty the Cat. As far as I'm concerned, I know very well why they named me Pussy Meow. She, the Human woman, has even explained in this handbook that my name is onomatopeic in origin. Onomatopeic: another big word whose meaning she is convinced is difficult for me, as if I didn't know that, according to her, it was I who suggested it to her with my meowing... Don't be ridiculous! The truth is that our dear two-footed friends are convinced that in the Man-Cat relationship, as they describe our association, it is they who have the upper hand; according to them, we limit ourselves to the most passive, ignorant acquiescence without being able to repay them in kind. In short, it doesn't even occur to them that we too have imagination, and that when we talk about them among ourselves, we use words, expressions and descriptions suitable to their lexicon. In fact, for us Cats, they are the No-Tails, the Two-Legged ones, the Bipeds or the Blah-Blahs. And naturally the Humans. Except when we label them (just as they are accustomed to labelling us) as pains in the neck when they annoy us, as two-bit tyrants when they insist on imposing their way of living on us, and as mawkish when they are overly sentimental with us. It amazes us, at times, how unjust they can be toward us, for example, when they doubt our comprehension and our intelligence with respect to their language. They do not realize that we, with our encyclopedic, ancestral store of knowledge, have filed away, along with our own everyday names, also those of other animals, such as dog, horse, butterfly, gecko, mouse and all the rest. And let it be said incidentally, and because it should be known, that we are capable of making sense of a good many human actions.

I went over her notes regarding Nebuchanezzar (see **The controversial expedience of big words**) *and had such a fit of hilarity that I had to roll around several times on the carpet to recover, while she, quite*

concerned, inquired: "What's come over you, roly-poly, my little roly-poly?" I replied: "Handbook, chiromancy, potpourri". I felt in the mood for wisecracks. But since I expressed myself in cat language, she didn't understand. Just as well: who knows how she would have reacted if she had realized she was being taken for a ride. She says that I'm the one who puts on airs but she, being a Human, is very full of herself.

Never let him know we suspect him

At this point we're certain of it: the Cat knows in what little esteem he was held (and is still held) from the collapse of the Middle Ages up to our own times.

Poor Pussycat, forever accused of being sly, two-faced and a born cheat. We ask ourselves, why do we always doubt him when we see him curled up in our favorite armchair, which is also his favorite? Nevertheless, our remorse was mitigated a little one day when we discovered our Pussy Meow intent on studying – with a furtive air – a string of pork sausages, arranged on the platter and ready to be served. Actually our mistrust had its origin back in time, the result of the impromptu, erratic behavior – which, by the way, was never repeated – of his predecessor, the chartreuse quadruped who had tyrannized us unscrupulously. One day he climbed up on the table and taking advantage of our distraction, took a string of sausages and went and hid it under the carpet, evidently thinking that he would eat them later on, away from the eyes of his busybody Humans. Not only that, but he pretended to be very surprised by our suspicions and accusations; he looked at us with the most innocent expression in the world when we demanded an explanation. Well, our Feline's attitude appeared so sincere that we began to doubt we had ever bought pork sausages. Only when the carpet was raised, during spring cleaning, did we discover that we had not been dreaming. But obviously the chartreuse had made himself scarce, holing up on the terrace, in his favorite pot. That's why when we caught our second Pussy Meow eying the sausages, we suspected a repeat of the episode, even though he doesn't like sausages.

Moral of the story: don't accuse the Cat of something you cannot prove.

Human culture: yuck!

Have you ever opened – you Humans who by chance can read us – an encyclopedic dictionary at the word "cat"? Try it and you will see that we are right, we poor martyrs, when we hold you responsible, all of you, for the adversities that we have had to overcome in order to finally gain recognition of our right to a place in the sun (only in the winter, fall and early spring, however, because after that it gets too hot and we prefer coolness and shade). You will find a quantity of insults to our dignity, in addition to a truly offensive lack of respect that is so evident that even the Human who is writing this little book with me has admitted it. First, however, I would like to state my opinion regarding the description "little book": I take the liberty of disagreeing with it because I consider the term too narrow, if only insofar as my contribution is concerned, which is not to be underestimated given the cognitive and scientific interest it holds.

According to the dictionary, the cat is generally considered a symbol of duplicity and of a tendency to steal: deceitful like a cat, theivish like a cat. "My personal experience" I've heard her, the Human, say, however, "has convinced me that if a cat steals, he doesn't do it because he's a... crook, but because he's hungry. That is, he behaves like any other animal". Including, I would add, the Two-Legged or No-Tail or Blah-Blah varieties.

Other expressions taken from the dictionary include: to see in the dark like cats, to play cat and mouse, to fight like cats and dogs, to cat around, to put the cat among the pigeons, and so on. A spiteful, witchy woman is also referred to as a cat, and fights among such females are called cat fights. As for getting along like cats and dogs, if it weren't for the fact that they, the Humans, foment rivalries and jealousies among us, behaving at times in ways which are very, very questionable, petting first one, then the other, praising the Cat when they want to spite the dog and viceversa, things would go a lot better between us. Another good one from the dictionary refers to the cat's tendency to isolate himself as if it were a misdemeanor. What does it mean? We Cats get along fine even by ourselves. That is to say, we don't need company, and it makes sense that we don't like to gather in big tribes. There's certainly nothing improper about living in regal solitude. Too bad they can't understand that.

"Not all black cats are witches". It's time to put a stop to this story about the witches' sabbaths and the bewitched trees,[1] meeting places for evil humanity. The Humans can't understand that they're not making us look good. With the excuse that we shared our existence with some poor old hag who had the misfortune to be branded a witch, they lost no opportunity to burn us. Question: what do you want to bet they'll want to roast us again?

On the contrary, they should treat us well. We're of distinguished lineage! And well they know it, so much so that they drew inspiration from our image, even in heraldry. There we are, in fact, on the shields. Some with ruffled fur and some with a rampant stance; one is fierce, another is sprinting off like an Olympic runner, and still another reposes, majestically seated on his hind quarters, his tail covering his front paws and – modestly – other parts. What a difference from the way dogs stretch out!

The name Cat is used in the building trade, in military arts *and in seamanship. Examples? As many as you want. The pile-driver's rammer is called a cat; the wooden pole with a three-pointed metallic star on top which at one time was inserted into cannon tubes to check if there were scratches is called a cat; in fortifications, a cat indicated a type of battering ram used to bring down the walls; in the nautical arena it was a kind of medieval ship, and in the ship's rigging the catwalk was the passage taken along the maintops of the mast. Also in naval jargon, the expression "cat's mooring" (that is, two-arms mooring) is used to designate a special way of mooring a ship with two anchors lowered at the bow. Perhaps the two-footed ones, especially the author of the present "little book" – there she goes again! – should be reminded of all this. Or perhaps a subtitle should be added, such as: "And Who Will Tell the Human?".*

[1] Our Pussy Meow, referring to bewitched trees, is obviously alluding to the walnut trees which, according to popular traditions as ancient as they are superstitious, would become, on certain nights, actual ball rooms for witches and sorcerers.

Even the shadows of the much maligned walnut tree were considered evil.

Lady Cats get it too

We have seen how our feline friend is justifiably mortified over the things which have been written (and are written) at his expense. Moreover, we had already mentioned this (see: **The controversial expedience of big words**), believing him to be more than justified in getting angry when he hears himself spoken about, since he suspects that we are always speaking ill of him, no matter what. Certain Humans, both in the past and in the present, have also directed the same kind of... `delicacies' toward Lady Cat. For example, "Kick the cat out; she'll come back sure enough." Or "The cat is honest when the meat is out of her reach." We feel it is even more difficult and impossible to apologize for this, especially when we recall the gentleness of female Cats whom we have known and loved in return. Sometimes a sense of justice prevails in the so-called popular wisdom, but say

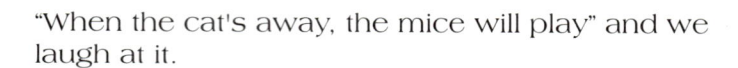

"When the cat's away, the mice will play" and we laugh at it.

And yet, there is no better compliment for a woman than to be told she has "intriguing cat's eyes". But would Lady Cat appreciate hearing: "You have beautiful Human's eyes"? I doubt it. Many Human males, when they are in love, find no better simile to murmur to their sweethearts than: "what a sweet little pussy cat's nose you've got". Never in fact "what a sweet little doggy's nose", unless they want to start an argument. As for the fashion model undulating down the runway, or a woman in the street with a striking figure, the ogling admirer will describe her as feline, not canine. And what about lovesick human sweethearts calling each other "Kitty" or "Kitten" or "Pussycat". Certainly not "Puppy" or "Little Dog". Assuming they want to keep the peace.

What can we say about skinning the Cat?

Lovely words, there's no denying it. But I repeat: "What can we say about skinning the Cat"? For one thing it doesn't seem right to harm a Cat, depriving her of the fur that the Good Lord gave her and which she did not procure on her own. Nor is it right that all too many female Humans spend huge amounts of money just to wrap themselves in the pelts of hapless animals whose only misfortune was that of having been well endowed at birth. Humans take care not to repeat certain expressions to our faces, convinced that we are unaware of them; as far as they are concerned "to skin a cat" means having to solve a difficult problem, one which stretches their abilities to the limit and may even have a detrimental outcome. In short, they admit that to skin a Cat may be an undertaking which is not only cruel but also counter-productive. And if they were to go and skin a lioness? I'd like to see them try! As for "Nervous as a Cat in a room full of rocking chairs" or "Cat got your tongue", I think they say these things because they attribute weakness to us – totally gratuitously – especially Lady Cats. I glanced at the title of this book: "Don't Tell the Cat". Right. It's best that they think about it a bit before opening their mouths, even though, when all is said and done, we're not so dangerous. Touchy? She maintains that this is so (see below: **Let's Be Cautious, Then**). *Yet their cautiousness puts us in a bad mood as well: all that tiptoeing around, as they say, is something we really can't begin to imagine, we who glide about with ease on our velvet paws. And this continuous speculation about what I do, about what they do, about what this means and what that means, also puts me in a bad mood. Enough, I'm sick of it. I hear her coming. I'll go and sharpen my claws on the beautiful carpet, which they, my Humans, prize very much.*

Annotations on the file

"Can you find the same number of analogies for the words 'dog' or 'horse', for example, as you can for the word Cat?" This question, too, was found on the computer, in the file dedicated to Pussy Meow, and the fingerprints on the keyboard were his. Just as the preceding annotations were his (we have put them all in italics for the convenience of the many readers His Majesty anticipates, as a result of his own precious contribution). Humility is really not his strong point. And there's more:

And then there's the cat herb or catnip (Nepeta cataria) that has an exciting influence on us Cats, like valerian. Its flowers are aromatic. I discovered a seedling of it growing wild in the garden of the house at the sea. I rubbed myself on it, brushing my muzzle, head and back over it until I crushed it.

Another dictionary term that concerns us is the cat-door: the opening at the bottom of a door used for

entry and exit by "His Majesty", as I am called more than once in this book. She should thank me for not having deleted the file! But two considerations stopped me: the first was that my Human (not she herself who doesn't understand much, if anything, about computers, but one of her nephews who is quite an expert with these gadgets) would succeed in recovering it; the second was fear of the dangerous threat of the word "cat-pokey". Just hearing this threat acts as a deterrent on me, or so they always say. The cat-pokey is the little room in which they confine me (only for a few minutes, actually, since they always quickly repent) when I am caught playing with the little jars of cream on her vanity table. That is, when caught red-handed, mouse in mouth... now isn't that witty.

Well then? We'll pretend we didn't notice these and other additions we fear we'll find in the future; better still we will incorporate his comments in our work – which isn't really work at all. We won't even scold our Pretty-Tail. Meanwhile we'll take note of the names he attributes to us. The name Blah-Blah mortified us a little, but how can we ask him for explanations? We'll let him get away with it though, because if he were to realize that he has contributed, he would be quite capable of demanding author's rights at the very least.

In a recent thriller by Patricia Cornwell, "Southern Cross", we came across a Cat accused one day of having manipulated the computer of his housemate, Virginia West, the Deputy Chief of the Richmond Police Force. Niles, an Abyssinian, was innocent, that time at least. All the same, it is agreed among us two-footed ones that whether deliberately or not, a Cat of a certain cultural level can, by accidentally walking on the keyboard or sitting down beside it intentionally, can indeed activate the commands of a computer. Which many Humans are barely able to do. Niles also knew how to dial the number of Virginia's ex-partner on the telephone, a man whom the Cat found quite *simpatico*. But that's another story.

We've given it some thought: we must find a way to keep Pussy Meow from accessing the file about himself. Knowing that the little meddler can stick his nose in it anytime he wants doesn't allow us to work in peace any more. Maybe it would be a good idea to actually forbid him to go near the computer at all. We suspect His Majesty is capable of opening a file on his own and unloading into it all the roguery that pops into his intelligent little head. We can actually visualize him half-closing his eyes to concentrate and find the most suitable words with which to lash our human customs.

A taboo topic par excellence: health

Another topic not to bring up directly with the Feline of the house has to do with his proverbial resistance to any illness, accidents or mishaps. "The Cat has nine lives". Nine or seven? There are two schools of thought about that, as they say pompously nowadays. For Latin cultures, the Cat has seven lives, while for Anglo-Saxons, he has nine. Whether seven or nine, the saying couldn't be more wrong. The Cat is subject to ill health and misfortunes just like all other living creatures, including Humans. Nevertheless, it is best that he remain unaware of the possibility of falling sick, since we consider him rather impressionable despite the fact that he doesn't complain when he suffers: a major difference between his species and ours. On the contrary, he

tends to go into hiding and conceal himself from our curiosity, even the most solicitous kind. Among other things, we think he places more faith in the therapeutic functions of Nature than in our own. It wasn't – or isn't – only the "cat-ladies" who believe in the longevity and robustness of their four-footed friends (perhaps because they are unjustly thought of as somewhat culturally naive). In a collection of essays and drawings on the world of cats, "Cat Catalog: Ultimate Cat Book", edited by Judy Fireman, there is the following citation, a classic of its kind: "It was Nature's Providence which gave this creature nine lives instead of one". And the number nines recurs – not merely a simple coincidence, we feel – in an expression used to describe an instrument of torture, "the cat-o'-nine-tails", a type of whip with exactly nine knotted leather cords, used in England at one time to flog criminals'. The instrument has only recently been abolished and sent to the archives, or more precisely, to the display cases of crime museums. A curious note: in Europe the same expression was used to indicate a type of scourge, made of ox nerves, and the Cossacks, who used and abused it, called it "knut".

Getting back to our quadrupeds' health, whoever shares a life with one of them knows how difficult it is to be in control, for the very reason that these little creatures are rather mistrustful. Unlike dogs, who have complete faith in their masters (accepting the fact that the Humans who take care of them are called "masters"), Cats are capable of rather testy reactions towards us when they are not feeling well. And yet, many vets and ethologists insist on advising us to feel our Cats' bodies frequently, perhaps camouflaging our endeavours with cuddles and caresses so as not to be categorically rejected. The purpose is to discover any possible abnormalities that may and should alarm us. In our opinion, it is hopeless to try to make the Cat cooperate. Even though particularly intelligent, he will act deaf if you try to explain the reason for your more or less clumsy attempts.

You know what can happen if you want to give him a simple injection, for example.

The vet describes an infallible method: "Prepare the

syringe and then squeeze your friend's skin between the thumb and index finger of your left hand up at his withers, where he will not feel the needle's prick or other discomfort". It sounds easy. Especially when Pretty-Tail tries to escape your praiseworthy intentions as you approach him with what he sees as a dangerous gadget, and with good reason. In such cases, it is best to stop him with a severe tone of voice, and let someone help you hold him still. A piece of advice: the needle must be short to avoid piercing the portion of skin straight through and sending the liquid squirting into the air.

Never say to him: let's go to the doctor

Never say to him: "Let's go to the vet". Especially when he doesn't appear to be in particularly good shape. Inevitably, the words will sound like a threat to him. All right, but even if we don't alert him, His Majesty – we've already agreed – will understand very well what is being schemed behind his back. The vet, though considerate and attentive, is not a likable figure to him. Nevertheless, although he detests his green coat, he is very fearful of him. So that, whenever possible, it is advisable to take the patient to the office, choosing to transport him there despite the problems it may pose, rather than scheduling a more comfortable (only for the Humans, that is) home visit. The surroundings may also affect the behavior of the sick Feline, terrifying rather than subduing him when he is served up on the table in the surgery.

Pussy Meow, for example, when he cannot escape the vet's hands, hides his little head under the arm of the Human who is with him. This is the only way he quiets down.

There are many procedures which are best performed by a vet: teeth cleaning, for example. And, obviously, vaccinations, setting fractures, and thorough visits with everything that goes with them. Wise vets, in fact, prefer to carry out teeth cleaning when a light anesthesia has already been administered to the Cat for other reasons. Nonetheless dry foods are rather useful for removing tartar and keep his teeth strong, not as an alternative, but as an integration with moist foods. Pussy Meow is a glutton for biscuit treats and would be capable of living on them exclusively if it weren't for his intestinal problems. Problems which occur when we're forced to keep him penned up in the house because of bad weather, preventing him from seeking out among the pots or flower beds the beneficial grass he knows better than an herbalist.

Never tell him "let's go to the doctor", then. Does the quadruped's distrust of green coats result from the sacrifice of his own physical efficiency, cruelly imposed on him to keep him from marking the home territory with the olfactory consequences that Feline owners are all well aware of? It is said that they don't remember anything about the operation they undergo. But how do we know? Especially when vets themselves affirm that the... memory of the procreation technique is not erased by the procedure.

Overly solicitous Human friends spend a lot of time in the waiting rooms of vets, holding the baskets containing their darlings on their laps, because they have been alarmed by strange phenomena, such as the anguished cries of their female Cat who has been going around the house plaintively wailing "mahohlooow". In such cases, it is natural to fear a terrible illness; but the She-Cat is merely love-sick. Or perhaps your Cat has spat up its food and you fear poisoning. Instead, it is simply a matter of having swallowed some fur, which the Feline expels by eaten voraciously in order to eliminate the bolus which, if retained too long, could have much more serious consequences.

A handsome ginger Cat, avid devourer of fish and tuna, was suffering from stomach and intestinal disturbances one day. The vet, reassuring the somewhat worried Human lady who had brought him there, prescribed a day of fasting, except for a few sips of tea. The Feline, seemingly absorbed in who knows what meditation, appeared not to have heard, much less understood. Once he got home, however, sidestepping and overtaking his Blah-Blah who was about to implement the instructions she had been given, he ran to his bowl quick as lightning and emptied it to the last crumb.

It is therefore hopeless to ask the apparently ailing Cat for a bit of cooperation. If he could express himself in our language, we would quickly realize that he was, in fact, sending us to the devil.

You're on your own

The trials which a quadruped's friend must face can be very trying, for example, when the Cat needs to be given medication. Generally, it is the vet who encourages the Human to administer it. As is the case with injections, the charge turns out to be quite a stressful business. Let's talk about it among ourselves a little, without letting the interested party overhear us.

How to give him a pill? Those who have attempted it know how energetically His Majesty will try to avoid swallowing it. Our experience has taught us that there are really very few Cats – you can count them on one hand – who will willingly agree to swallow the nasty thing which is put in their mouth. The majority of them spit it back out. You can therefore try a trick which sometimes works, namely, mixing the tablet with a little of his favorite food. The Cat will eat a small mouthful and right afterwards will produce a series of gags to vomit it back up, but without success; the second time you administer the pill, he won't fall for it, and will push the human hand away with the same gesture that he generally uses to cover up his excrement. Then, once he becomes fully familiar with certain manoeuvers, he will begin to play a clever game, licking the pill clean and leaving it on display in his bowl. Tail held high, he will walk away haughtily, without a word. Yet you can read in his demeanor words which make us lose face: "There, you thought you would put one over on me?". At this point, it is necessary to resort to more drastic, as well as complicated, measures:

1) Wrap Pretty-Tail in a towel;
2) Hold his paws still, especially his front paws;
3) Pick him up in your arms;
4) Make him open his mouth. How? By pushing into the corners of it with your thumb and index finger, applying a gentle yet firm pressure;
5) When the Cat has opened his mouth, lift his head a little;
6) Quickly place the tablet in the back of his mouth;

7) Close the creature's jaws immediately and hold them shut until he has swallowed. If he doesn't want to, blow on his muzzle as if you too were a Cat. Surprise, surprise, he will swallow the pill.

Other medicines. If on the other hand you have to make him take a liquid medicine, the operation may be simplified by using an eyedropper bent so that it can be inserted into the corner of his mouth to make it easier for him.

And what about injections? The intravenous ones should be left to the vet, of course. The others have already been discussed (see: **A taboo topic par excellence: health**).

Inhalers. These operations are very disagreeable to His Majesty. In order to have some chance of success, it is a good idea to force the patient to enter his little carrying case or a cage, bringing the inhalator's nozzle as close as possible to the bars, in the direction of his little nose. Our impertinent Pussy

Meow, as soon as he hears the hiss of the inhaler, turns around so that his posterior gets the benefit of it.

It is wise to keep in mind that Cats are like children: they love to be cuddled, but they're afraid of the hand that feeds them. Cajoling them with your voice, encouraging them, praising them, scolding them if needed, can be helpful.

Ok, let's speak of health

It makes me angry when the Humans in my house try to take me for a fool. They thought I wouldn't be able to get into the study and use the computer, and they had actually left it turned on, so certain were they of having put one over on me. But I, Pussy Meow, can open any door, provided it's not one of those heavy ones, reinforced with some devilry on the inside, or locked with a key. And I've given them ample proof of it by actually opening the front door of the house at the sea, arousing the utmost astonishment of a friend of theirs who was very skeptical about my abilities. But there again, what does the old French proverb say? "There's no workman who can construct a door that can keep out a cat or a lover".

So then, where did we leave off last time? We were talking about the rumors and idiotic things said about us, regarding our alleged resistance to physical complaints. There's an old English proverb which

treats female Humans the same way. "A woman – it says – has nine lives like a cat". What's good for the goose, as they say... But how have they been able to establish that Cats and women have hearty constitutions? Have they forced women, too, into laboratory pens and subjected them to the same abuses – which they call studies – that they subject us to, and to which legislators and animal rights activists close a blind eye? Have they conducted the same experiments – for which they should be ashamed – on them? And then they have the gall to brag and write about them! They say they are "reporting". My Human often recalls an episode concerning a little female cat, which gives me the willies. She even mentioned it in an earlier handbook about Cats, which I think was entitled "How To Obey Your Cat". Well, this poor creature was being subjected to a continuous flow of gas at the laboratory where she was held prisoner. They would dispatch it to her through a little opening made in the enclosure in which she spent her miserable life. But sooner or later the gentle little Cat became aware of where that evil flow was coming from, and as soon as she noticed the hiss, she would block the opening with her paw. The experimenters pardoned her. How noble of them. They have also studied at length the reason why, when we Cats fall, we are able to land on all four paws without – they say – hurting ourselves much, especially as the cushioned pads on our paws soften the impact. That's not to say, however, that the manoeuvre always turns out well, especially if we plunge down some several dozen feet! It seems that even when falling back down, we have the agility to turn around during the descent. Now isn't that something! Nevertheless, it's preferable not to put it to the test.

According to the writer Mark Twain, one of the most important differences between a cat and a lie is that a cat has only nine lives. I've also heard this from one of my Humans, who added that she was puzzled by the redundancy of so many adages – she calls them claptrap – especially when, on the roadways, you come across the mangled carcasses of what were – she says – marvellous little living creatures.

Top secret... It goes without saying

Why absolute top secret? In our relationship with Mister Cat or Lady Cat, we have tried to explain to ourselves the reasons for their mistrust of us when we try to help them. Although they seem to ask for our help when they are in difficulty, it is soon clear that they must make an enormous effort to put themselves completely in our hands. It's a strange sentiment that they share with all other animals, there's no denying it. They attribute to us – rightly so, but who told them? – a loss of instinct: that impulse uncontrolled by conscience, which at one time was natural and hereditary, and which should guide our actions, but doesn't any more. It is instinct to which they entrust the job of perpetuating the species, and they are doubtful whether our actions, conscious rather than instinctive,

can be right; they don't know what it is that guides our actions, since reasoning – of which we are so proud and to which we ascribe our behavior – is unknown to them. Nor does their comprehension take into account the experience we've acquired, whereas they have no uncertainties about their own. "A scalded cat dreads even cold water". So says the umpteenth maxim, more or less. Nonetheless, whether His Majesty trusts us or tries to rebel against our attentions, we should still behave shrewdly, disguising our salutary reconnoiterings of his body with caresses – reconnoiterings which the vets recommend be done on a weekly basis. Kenneth Anderson, one of the best known ethologists, has written, in fact, that the most effective preventive medicine for a Cat consists in weekly "home visits", advising the Human on what procedure to follow, namely, feeling the cat from head to toe. Through such methodical observation he will come to know his little creature well enough to be able to make an early discovery of anything wrong, and thereby prevent greater problems. Here is a simple list of examinations which even those Humans least experienced in medicine can perform without annoying their feline friend:

Eyes. Get into the habit of looking into your friend's eyes. If they are opaque and lack their usual lustre, it means that your Cat is sickening for something. There is even greater reason to worry if the eye is covered by a so-called third eyelid. If instead there's something in the corner of the eye, don't worry about it; it's nothing serious. The trouble can be removed by delicately wiping the area with a piece of cloth or a tissue.

Ears. They must always be kept clean. When the Cat shakes his head, he is actually getting rid of insects, blades of grass, little leaves or anything else he may pick up from the plants as he wanders about the garden or balcony. The care of the ears is so important that when Cats live in tribes, you will see them taking turns cleaning one another's ears. The Human, who becomes the substitute for mama Cat or another four-footed companion, should arm herself – so to speak – with a wad of cotton to wipe the internal part of the auricle. If an unpleasant odor is noticed or if the wad of cotton turns brown during the process, or if the Cat frequently shakes his head or bends his ears, he may have contracted otitis or be troubled by a parasite. Our advice is to take him to the vet without waiting too long.

<u>Teeth</u>. Although many vets maintain it is a good habit to have tartar removed in the office, the Cat can take care of cleaning his own teeth by chewing dry food, as already mentioned. For this reason, it is advisable to always put some dry treats within reach of... his teeth. And keep a bowl of fresh water nearby, since the so-called biscuits will make the Cat thirsty; he needs to wash the dry food down with frequent sips of water otherwise it may do him more harm than good. Still, checking our friend's mouth, or rather the inside of his mouth, is another task to place on the list of treatments required to keep him healthy. An unpleasant odor that persists and is not due to something he has eaten – fish, for example – together with a coating on his teeth and too much saliva can indicate that there is tooth decay or something else needing treatment.

<u>Claws</u>. When the quadruped scratches the barks of trees, or worse yet the covering of a seat or armchair,

he is sharpening his own weapons. Generally the procedure is completed by using his teeth. No, he doesn't tear out his claws, as the inexperienced might suspect and worry about. Our friend only removes the useless part of his claws, encouraging regrowth. To avoid problems with the carpets in our homes, it might be advisable to clip his claws, but only those of the front paws. It is mortifying to the Cat, but at certain times it is necessary for both Cat and Human to give and take a bit. Although one can learn to do it oneself, it is best to have the vets cut his claws. In any case, special small clippers should be used, not the scissors we employ for our own grooming needs; then too, only the curved tip of the claw should be trimmed to avoid damaging the nerve or causing a painful infection.

Coat. Vets recommend careful cleaning of the coat. One of the most troublesome complaints that can strike our four-footed friend is eczema. This is indicated by the appearance of small red spots on the skin, which then become little blisters; the blisters, which secrete serous fluid and give off an unpleasant odor, in

55

turn form scabs. According to the experts, eczema is a skin inflammation caused by an imbalance in the diet, for example, an excess of starchy foods. Since the itching caused by eczema is not only intense but also persistent, the animal continues to scratch himself, thereby losing his fur. How can you remedy this condition? Whether or not the interested party protests or accepts your attentions with resignation, his entire coat must be washed with warm water to which a few grams of alum have been added. Once he has been dried with a warm towel, the blisters will break and must then be treated with penicillin or other medicinal desiccant in powder form, which can easily be found in any pharmacy stocking veterinary products. In addition, the Human will have to prevent his feline friend from licking his skin. Ethologist Angelo Lombardi wrote that the ideal solution would be to put the patient in a sack, leaving only his head free. Today's remedies are less drastic, one of which consists of a large collar, jokingly called a lampshade, which it resembles, and which prevents the unfortunate victim from twisting his head backwards.

Make him beautiful? Yes, but...

Brushing. Although the procedure is necessary, it is not a good idea to announce to your Cat your intention to pick up a brush, saying to him as we are generally tempted to do: "Come here, your coat is all tangled; look at that, you even have knots. How can you stand it? Sure, you think all you have to do is wash yourself, but you don't untangle the knots, and moreover with that little tongue of yours that absorbs everything, you accumulate a fine mass in your stomach. Then you feel sick, you vomit, and I have to clean it up". Instead, slip his brush into your pocket or put it behind your back or wherever, waiting for the right moment to use it. As for "his brush"... he would very willingly do without such a possession, so much so that if it should fall into his claws, goodbye brush!

If he can't destroy it, he will surely hide it in certain little nooks which only he knows about, and you will only be able to find it during spring cleaning or other major house cleaning stints. The Cat doesn't appreciate having the Human take care of his coat, that's for certain. Yet our care can have positive results in that it allows us to ensure, first of all, that his beautiful fur does not shelter undesirable guests. In addition, as already mentioned, the brush or comb removes superfluous hair, thereby preventing our quadruped from swallowing it. What kind of brush should be used? There are various types sold in specialty shops. However, it's best to select one whose bristles are neither too delicate nor too rough. The best ones are actually those with metallic bristles, the kind which many Humans use for their own grooming. And the comb most suitable for untangling knots should be made of aluminum. Long-haired Cats require daily brushing and combing. Even if they try to resist and are explicit in showing how unwilling they are to endure what they evidently consider a whim on the part of their Human, they will

59

eventually accept the operation without too much ado, especially if you take care to have them stretch out on a cloth or towel which has been warmed on the radiator. As you run the brush along his fur with one hand, pet the little creature with the other, encouraging him and even praising him for his good will; only at the end should a few little strokes be given against the fur, though never with shorthair breeds. The Cat should not be made to feel that the operation is a show of force, a Human whim or a punishment, but rather an expression of loving concern. Siamese, chartreuse, and even tabby cats having little fur on their undersides can also do without the use of the brush, since a single stroke, performed carelessly, could cause irritation. Perfectionists complete the operation by applying a warm, damp cloth, a little like the ones they offer on top American domestic airlines to passengers who have spent the night on board a red-eye flight.

Bath. The feline's aversion to water is well known. To convince a Cat to let himself be bathed is a hopeless undertaking to say the least. And yet our four-footed friend is one of the cleanest creatures. Thanks to his rough little tongue, he is able to remove all impurities from his fur. If you really insist on bathing him, it is best to resort to sponge baths (essential if he has skin problems), drying him carefully afterwards. This is another procedure which is difficult to carry out. His Majesty detests the hairdryer because of the blowing, which despite its warmth, sounds menacing just the same. Rubbing him thoroughly with a towel is the only solution. The operation, however, lasts only as long as the party in question allows it.

Parasite control. The Cat is immune to ticks ensconcing themselves in his coat. Fortunately. But, he can be attacked by fleas, lice and various mites. Have no fear, they do not transfer themselves to human skin, even though the Cat may scratch furiously in an attempt to alleviate the discomfort they cause him. At one time, the treatment consisted of sprinkling his coat with an powder insecticide, specifically designed for animals. Today in drugstores you can buy phials containing a liquid product to be sprinkled on his withers: in other words, where the back and neck join. This treatment is preferable as it avoids the risk of His Majesty poisoning himself by trying to lick the powder off his fur. A warning, which is also printed on the package: the liquid is to be applied to the skin and not to the coat, and only in a very restricted area. In order to be effective, the procedure must generally be repeated every two months. The Cat who raised hell to avoid it at the time of the first application, will find it so beneficial that he will subsequently be... consenting and will not try to get away, even if his Human does not repeat the explanations given to him the first time.

63

Words are not superfluous

At times, asking the Cat: "Do you want to eat?" may seem superfluous. Those who know little or nothing about felines will think, what good is it? Those who are familiar with cats know very well that if His Majesty wants to eat and his bowls are empty, he will clearly make himself understood. How? He will sit in front of the refrigerator or the cupboard where his food is kept and protest loudly against those who are trying to starve him to death. Or if he does not find you within range, he will go and call you and guide you to where he wants you. His manoeuvering goes like this: he will stare at you, communicate his hunger by meowing, and then invite you to follow him by zigzagging in front of you with a springy step that not even Elvis Presley could perform; in doing so he also runs the risk of tripping you and being left without food. And yet... and yet, why not attempt an exchange with your friend. It can be really amusing, I can assure you from experience. For instance, if you ask him "Do you want to eat?", Pussy Meow, might well reply with a yowl which is not merely an affirmative, but much, much more than that. "Marrammamaoh ah ah!", he complains, accompanying his alleged suffering with two or three yawns: mouth wide open to the ears, clearly revealing his miniature tiger's teeth. "Marrammamaoh ah ah", as we wrote earlier (see *What Did The Cat Say?*, published by Gremese) can be translated something like this: "So you're hard of hearing, huh?". In that same handbook-dictionary, we gave an example featuring one of the family ginger toms. In fact, we added: "Paco resorts to an even more convincing technique. He takes his plate between his teeth and bangs it on the floor. It is a habit he acquired when he was very little, and he surrenders to the temptation to perform it sadistically during the night".

Nevertheless, when Pretty-Tail refuses to eat food he doesn't like, even though it's been prescribed by the vet, it is not only superfluous but useless to try to persuade him by saying "Go on, it's good for you, it will make you better", or to admonish him with "Think about how many poor creatures have nothing to fill their stomachs and are rummaging in the trash bins at this very moment...". You could also reproach him with the fact that there are many Human children currently suffering from hunger in the world, who would eagerly devour the food which a capricious little creature like you turns his nose up at. If his tummy is full, he will act deaf and unperturbably go on pretending to cover his bowl with imaginary earth, as though it were a heap of refuse.

In such cases, vets and ethologists are right when they preach: "Leave him to his caprices and let him go hungry. He'll eat when his stomach complains".

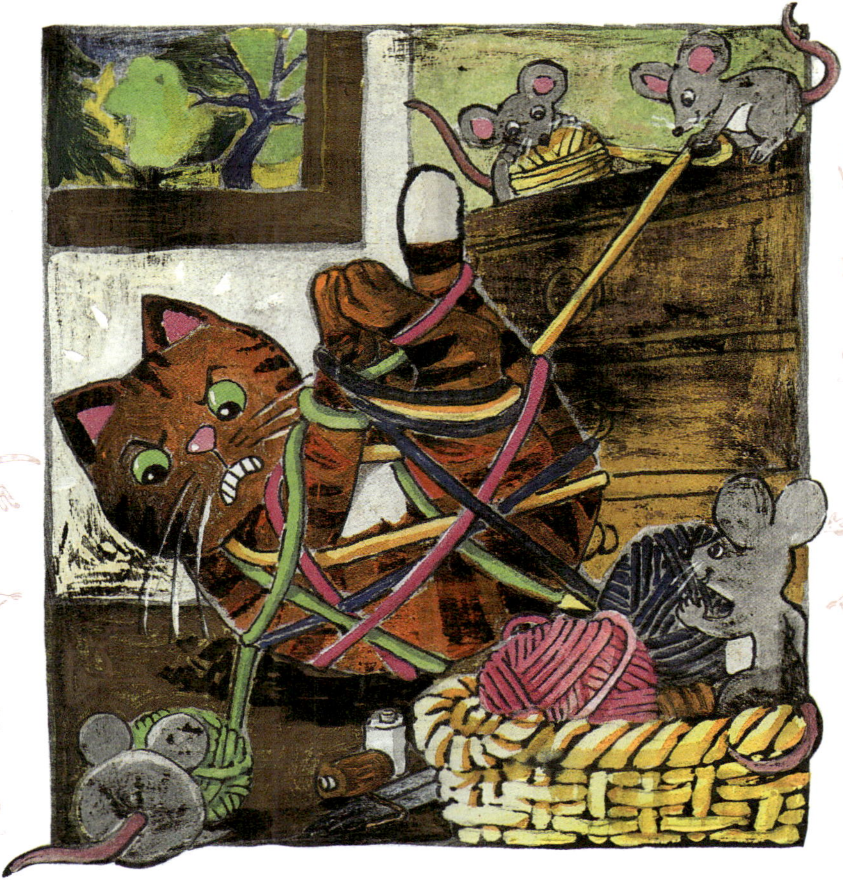

Let's keep it a secret still

<u>Trips</u>. Pussy Meow does not exactly go willingly into his carrying case. When he notices preparations for moving from the house in the city to the one at the sea, he makes various attempts to get out of it. The most frequent is that of crouching under one of the lowest beds and pushing himself against the wall until he is practically stuck to it, making it very difficult to reach him. Nonethess we have found that all we have to do is say to him: "Okay, fine, we'll go away and leave you here by yourself for days, without food" and he will crawl out on his belly and let himself be caught. Still, he will sulk for a good part of the trip if we are traveling by car. We never know if it's because we forced him to come or because of the threats which preceded the use of force. Agreed, it would be better not to make threats, given the touchiness of the subject in question. And yet, a poor Human must take some action if he is to enjoy sharing the joys and anxieties of a trip with a friend.

Pussy Meow, once his bad mood has passed, even participates in his family's protests and reactions against the abuses of other road users, howling curses and imprecations in the feline tongue.

One summer evening in New York, during a particularly sultry smmer, we were at Kennedy Airport waiting to retrieve our baggage which had taken an entirely different route (things are truly the same the whole world over). Thus we were able to watch a number of Cats returning from vacation in their sturdy carrying cases, the kind suitable for such trips; it was really an exraordinary sight. They arrived on the rotating conveyer belt, mixed in with bags and suitcases, since animals generally travel in pressurized holds. We were struck by both the indifferent attitude of their owners, who didn't have a word of praise for their friends, as well as by that of the Felines. Both seemed to be trying not to look at one another. What words had they exchanged before going on board? Then the story told by Peter Gethers, "The Cat Who Went to Paris", came to mind. In the book, Gethers, publisher, novelist and film expert, assures us that he usually carries Norton with him in a big hand bag, as carry-on luggage. And since he pays for a ticket for Norton as well, he doesn't let the protests of the crew members get the better of him, but insists that the bag containing his feline friend be kept beside him. What are we going to do about the inflexible regulations regarding felines, we ask ourselves each time we think about it. Maybe the Cat travelers that summer evening in New York appeared angry for good reason due to this and who knows how many other instances of discrimination.

<u>Give him company</u>. The house Cat doesn't always need to share the comforts of a roof and a ready meal with one of his own kind. Our Pussy Meow, for example, is rather jealous, not only of his territory but also of his Humans, whom he considers his exclusive property. In this he is not at all unique. Among us Blah-Blahs, there are those who share their life with two or even more cats, but in such cases, in our humble opinion, it is likely that they have recreated – on the terrace, in the garden, in the living room – the typical environmental conditions of a feline clan, limiting their

71

own role to that of complying with their guests' needs. Otherwise, life together could might sometimes be far from idyllic. Still, if you want to have two Cats in the house, it is best to think about it in advance, and acquire them at the same time. That way, by growing up together, the feline will not resent the intrusion of another presence in his world.

In fact, the Cat who is accustomed to being the only little king in a family, gets used to considering Humans as his own kind and to regulating his own behavior according to their standard; he virtually renounces the animal condition. From among his Humans, then, he chooses one who can subsitute for mama Cat, whether that person be male or female. While this may arouse in the chosen one great feelings of tenderness, it also obligates that person to attend to him, take care of him, always give him food which he likes, allow him to sleep at her feet or beside her, and so on. In the latter case, the person will have to guard against His Majesty's purring and its consequences without, however, wounding him, since a feline's sensitivity is very vulnerable.

Colette, the well-known French writer, wrote that when a Cat purrrs it is as if he were kneading flour and water, that is, making dough. As the Feline unsheathes and retracts his claws, there is the risk he may leave rather painful marks on the Human's skin, just as a cheese grater might do.

Parking Him During Vacation. Personally we are against leaving Pussy Meow even for a limited period of time, let alone a month's vacation. True, there are excellent boarding houses for Cats and dogs, maintained by reliable people. But try and make your feline friends understand that you haven't abandoned them. It's useless to repeat it to them as you accompany them into... exile. At least respect their dignity by being silent. However, it is well to keep in mind that many hotels have no problem accepting domestic animals accompanying their Humans. You can even take them on ships. Nevertheless, if you have to go abroad for a short time, then you should leave the Cat at home, since otherwise he would have to undergo vaccinations and, in some countries, be placed in quarantine.

Beauty contests: what a drag

There is a female Cat whom I have often observed strutting about in the sun on the terrace that borders ours. From the airs she puts on, she seems to be well aware of having descended from aristocratic stock. A pretentious type, all fur, and white; a little voice full of arrogance. Once when she dared to come too close to my territory, I tried to clout her through a space in the glass that acts as a divider. Who cares that she's a female! How dare she attempt to trespass on others' property? She wailed her complaint so loudly that it made both her Human and mine come running and they started the same old story, the same old tune... You know how it goes, right? You know what Humans are like. The one from over there consoling Her Offended Dignity: "My sweet little treasure, what did the bad boy do to you?". The one on this side saying to me: "Aren't you ashamed of yourself, mistreating such a beautiful little creature?". And then, though without

75

being able to see each other very well through the opaque glass: "Please forgive him". "No, no, it's nothing, right Pincess?". Her name is Princess, that one there. It was on that occasion that we learned about the lofty lineage from which the victim of my ignorance had descended, and even had to sit through a list of her credits: recognition of her beauty, acknowledgment of her purebred status, and a string of contests and competitions in which she had competed.

Since that time, the two Human ladies have become friends, and regularly exchange opinions and advice about us. For my part, whenever I see the pincess's profile through the glass, I continue my efforts to swat her with my paw. Just once. Just one swipe.

Her Human – even more pretentious than her Cat – has also told us how much care, and what kind, is required so that princess – with a small "p", that's how I choose to write it – may display herself in top form on the runways and ramps. Who does she think she is, a different colored Naomi Campbell! Brushing, styling, embellishing her with ribbons, special talcum powders and sponge baths and hot cloths. What a drag! It's a good thing I was born a mongrel.

"But you're beautiful just the same" my Blah-Blah tells me over and over again "even though you're not a purebred!". And when she thinks that I feel particularly mortified at not having decorations and pedigrees, she consoles me by saying: "My poor little cat, which competition could I enter you in, fat as you've become, and a little hunchbacked to boot. And that tail with the broken tip?". At times she speaks in a sing-song. Then, sighing, she adds: "And yet I wouldn't trade you even for a Persian…". Now I ask you, are these the things you should say to a Cat who is already humiliated enough by having to share his space with such a conceited presence …? Why doesn't my biped keep quiet? Anyway, their contests and competitions don't matter a whit to me. Then, too, if I think about all the sessions that someone of my mixed breed status would have to undergo in order to improve his appearance, to make his coat and eyes shine and his teeth white, well, I consider myself fortunate to be the way I am. Isn't my No-Tail friend the very one who tells everyone within earshot that true beauty is internal?

They don't need words

So then, we can save our breath. Our Cats understand us even without words, as though they were reading our thoughts. We have ascertained this by attentively observing the various feline friends to whom we offer, or have offered, our hospitality – or to those who have demanded it, without standing on ceremony. In exchange they give us the attention and regard which Humans would never think of extending even to the most beloved of their own kind, all without having to call attention to it with big or fancy words. Our Pussy Meow, for example, gives us proof of his tenderness and sensitivity each and every day, even though he's a bit of a grumbler as you can see by these notes, written by his own two paws in addition to our two hands.

Sifting through our memories, we can't help but marvel once again as we recall the behavior of a little female Cat whom we had taken into our home in very poor shape. She expressed her gratefulness in a

79

number of ways, but without toadying to us as a Human might have done in her place. She was very attached to the Cat who was the current tyrant in our family but who, having been neutered, considered her barely worthy of his attention. In fact, he actually mistreated her in a quite detestable way. Yet when he fell gravely ill, she quickly understood that he would not come out of it, and we feared she would make him pay for the tyrannies and oppressions he had subjected her to. Later, however, we regretted having misjudged her generosity. Contrary to our expectations, she did all she could to make his condition easier by not giving him the least bit of bother. She got to the point where she no longer went to lie down beside him, nor did she climb up on the beds, or on the armchairs, or in the big pot on the terrace, as she used to do when she wanted to assert her own right to also enjoy certain comforts. She didn't let him out of her sight, and seemed almost ready to run to his aid, had he asked her to. And when the Cat had passed away, after having looked for him in all his favorite spots, not wanting to accept the evidence right up until the end, she too departed this life.

For many years, a handsome ginger Cat was forced to accept living with a German Shepherd who, on the contrary, wanted nothing to do with him. In order to keep the peace, their Humans made one of them stay on the upper floor of the house and the other on the lower floor, which had a little terrace. When the old dog died – though far away from the dwelling they shared – the Cat let a few days go by before he at last descended from the upper floor and went to crouch on the back of the armchair where his disconsolate mistress was sitting. From that time on, whenever he saw his Blah-Blah absorbed or saddened, he would go to her and – turning up the volume of his purring – offer his little head for a kiss, tickle her face with his whiskers, or stick his little snout near her ear. In short, he put all his consolatory capabilities into action. At times he even tried to substitute for his old friend-enemy by putting himself on guard in front of the doorway of the house. Or he would try to inspect the table or sink by standing up on his hind legs, as the dog used to do. He could easily have jumped up there on all fours but he didn't; we think it's because he wanted us to actually forget that he was simply a Cat. Simply sweet and gentle.

Our four-footed friends, then, respect pain and suffering, human or otherwise. We continue to repeat it without fear of being boring because it is something that is a source of continual amazement to us. It is why we like to recall how the chartreuse Cat, our companion for sixteen years, took to consoling one of his Humans at a time of grave concern by trying to... dry her tears with his little tongue.

There is only one occasion when Pretty-Tail seems to ignore us, ignore the house, and ignore the family which he has done everything possible to become a full-fledged member of. That's when love-madness tempts him to the point of making him lose his head, as young people say today. Amorous playfulness, in fact, leads Cats to perform foolhardy feats of fancy, like when they launch into crazy races, for example, respecting nothing and no one: neither a Human who is ill, let's suppose, nor their own safety.

Natalia Ginzburg, in one of her books, told about

83

how her beautiful Persian female ran out on the rooftops in pursuit of a feline Don Juan on the make, rolling with him into the street and ending in a romantically exciting way an existence which up till then had been serene but monotonous. In another mad race, the Cat of an acquaintance of ours flew out a top floor window. Though he didn't tell us what he was feeling, in that particular case, we suspected – given an experience we had with one of our own quadrupeds – the reason was a painful stomach ache due to a mistaken diet, such as a gluttonous meal or too much of the grass which so whets the feline's palate.

When we took in Pussy Meow because he was sick, we told his mother who was watching over him: "We'll treat him well, we'll have him taken care of, don't worry". She looked at us fixedly. With just one look of her beautiful lake-blue eyes she wanted to assure us that we had her entire trust. Even before hearing our words, she had understood our intentions. Her eyes seemed to say: "Don't waste your words. I know you are friends".

P.S. I'm quite sure that at this point in her writings the Human co-author of the present... essay, was genuinely moved. Just as I'm quite sure that the reason she mentioned my real mother and the moment she took me from her was because – as the saying goes – one speaks to the daughter-in-law so that mother-in-law gets the message. In this case, the mother-in-law would be me. O.K., then, I've got the message. Signed: Pussy Meow. Oh, and by the way, I'm not going to give up writing.

For your own good, don't dare say certain things

Four-legs is fidgeting restlessly around you, meowing and meowing. You ask him: "What do you want? I gave you food and water; you've done your business. Well then? You've even been out on the balcony; don't forget that, and don't forget that it was you who wanted to come back in. So now what's wrong?".

He will respond in his own way by coming closer and closer to the couch where you are relaxing, reading or watching a TV program. Finally you try asking: "Do you want to come up here, by any chance?".

"Ahah ahah ahaah" he meows, running it all together without commas, since he doesn't have much regard for punctuation. Yes, you understood him just fine. Affirmative: either you move over or else surrender your place to him. If it's a cold day, and the heaters are turned

87

down or not working well, once on board His Majesty will also demand to be wrapped in something. In this case, your robe.

His and your vital space. When your Cat first enters your house, don't even think about saying to him: "Make yourself at home. From now on you're one of us". He will take you literally. To begin with he will compete with you for possession of your bed, far more comfortable than the padded basket you've provided for him; next he will attempt the comfort of your favorite armchair. At first, with a misleading little call such as "meeahrr meeayrr", he will politely ask that you make a little room for him. Touched by this, you will squeeze up against the edge of the chair a little and he will settle himself next to you, ending up conquering your heart with his satisfied purring. You'll pet him and he will give you a little nudge with his behind – pointing out the cramped space you've allowed him – to make you move over a little bit more. Since you can neither slim down just like that, nor give up your vital space completely, you don't pay any attention to him. You will regret it. His Majesty will move on to more substantial manoeuvres, the first phase of which will consist of solidly planting his four paws against the back of the chair. The second phase will involve robustly shoving his back against yours, so that you will end up on the very edge of the chair. "Is that any way to act?" you will say then, and he will answer with a "Mmammammah" of undisputed significance, namely: "You could also move somewhere else".

A place at the table. Generally speaking, common Cats – that is, those who do not belong to your clan but who during the summer, or on days when the weather is fine, come and visit in your garden – arrive when you are about to sit down at the table and sit politely next to the chair of this or that guest, guided by an instinct which suggests to them which of the table companions may be the most munificent. They sit politely and wait. The house Cat, on the other hand, quickly secures his own place on a chair, to keep an eye on the table and on the food which is being served. How? By making his Humans understand that he for one is different from other quadrupeds, those without a regular home and without a birthright. He is a member of the family and has the same rights as family members – rights which have been acknowledged by everyone. Included in the bill of rights is that of a reserved chair. A chair which will always be the same, and which will always be located in the same place, at the same distance from the table. Once seated, His Majesty will stretch his muzzle out every now and then, apparently to delight in the aromas, though actually to scrape up a morsel of something good from some merciful hand: a tidbit which he will then sniff, lick and swallow with his eyes closed blissfully.

His terrace or his garden. Here there is no competition with the Human. On the contrary, it is much appreciated if the latter escorts His Majesty in his wanderings among the bushes or from one pot to another, in search of the little plant which is sheer bliss to the Cat's palate. Competition, if any, develops and explodes only if there happens to be a trace of a strange Cat or dog in the vicinity. For His Majesty, the terrace, balcony and garden are part of his rightful territory over which he is

91

determined to reign supreme. In order to succeed in his legitimate objective, in the teeth of any possible usurpers, he marks these areas over and over again. That is, if he is still intact and has not been subjected to that cruel practice which is nonetheless necessary for his and our tranquility, namely, castration.

His house. At one time it was said that Cats become attached to the house and not to the Humans who dwell in it. This is not true. When our Cats are left alone for a time, they get sulky and make us pay for it. Our Cats wait behind the door for us to come back; they recognize the sound of our steps, without ever being mistaken. They have mastered both our city house and the one at the sea. They recognize every corner of both, and even when they've been away for some time, they show no hesitation at finding their way to the place where their things are usually kept: litter box and food and water bowls. The same rules governing the exclusiveness of their territory apply to the house as well.

Yes, the quadruped does become attached to the house into which he is accepted, but he loves his

Humans too. He is capable of loving. Something which Blah-Blahs are not always capable of.

His freedom. This, alias poor Cat, we deny him or limit. Egotistically we do it to keep him close to us, take comfort in his purring, delight in observing his wild or funny games, and marvel at his creative fancy. But above all we do it with the intention – though this is no excuse – of safeguarding him from dangers he might encounter if we were to leave him free to roam about freely. And yet... and yet:

"Do you think that I would change
my present freedom to range
for a castle or moated grange?
wotthehell wotthehell"

That's what our Feline thinks, too. At least so we are told by Mehitabel, the alley-cat princess-poetess of Don Marquis' "Archy and Mehitabel".

And to think, all of these observations sprang from a: "Pray, Sire, make yourself at home here with us".

Feline enigma

Who knows what "cute little title" my Human will give to the annotations which follow...

Annotations which concern a new Human theory, namely, that if a Cat is the only feline sharing a family's life, he will soon learn to communicate with the family members in a most efficient way, behaving in a positively logical and rational manner. Why? They explain it by using the example of a Human forced to live abroad without knowing the language of the foreign country. Such a person would have to learn the language as quickly as possible otherwise he would be cut off from the community. Similarly we Cats, finding ourselves in... an absolute minority among the bipeds, would adjust by mimicking their behavior; in other words, we would try to communicate on the same level. An explanation which, obviously, doesn't please me. According to the rule of par condicio, they too should have to imitate

us. If they want to communicate better, they should have to learn to meow, walk on all fours, and purr. On the other hand, the theory continues, if they were to impose a companion of our own species on us, then *we would go back to being part of a clan, regressing to an... animal condition.*

The Human lady, with whom I'm writing this little book, disagrees with current opinions which condemn the alleged humanization of domestic animals. She says that its advocates don't want to see us progress. As though one could prevent any type of progress, including that of animals. She therefore feels authorized to advise persons living alone who seek comfort and affection not to keep more than one Cat. Sifting through her comments, I came across these words: "The Cat, deprived of his wanderings and removed from his natural habitat, needs man, and makes him his accomplice and brother *(sic!)*. His ability to adapt, which has enabled him to come through so many adversities, if not unharmed, in the end victorious, still plays a prominent role in his nature. Nevertheless, even in a clan – whether it be large or small – the element of unselfish devotion which he reserves for his Human sometimes comes to the fore and he willingly sets himself apart from the group. Who knows for what reason. Feline mysteries!".

Poets and bards for sir and lady Cat

I have a cat
her name is Tit
and by the fire
she loves to sit.

We tried to recite this ingenuous little poem to Pussy Meow using the intonation of a British child, having learned it at an early age from a little book in English. It did not move him. So, since he's an Italian Cat, we tranlated it for him:

Io ho una gatta
il suo nome è Tit
e vicino al fuoco
le piace starsene seduta.

He looked at us through half-closed eyes: one of his habits to let us know if – and how much – a gift is appreciated. "Ah, so you like poetry?" we asked him with the insinuating tone we use with him when we are able to guess his feelings. Thus, seeing we were on fairly safe ground, we continued by reciting in his honor the old popular nursery rhyme which goes like this:

If I lost my little cat, I would be so sad;
I would ask St. Jerome what to do to be glad.
I would ask St. Jerome, just because of that,
For he's the only saint I know who kept a kitty cat.

He purred, gave us a nudge with his head as he usually does to show his affection, and led us in the direction of his bowl to show us how desperately empty it was.

Why Saint Jerome? Because it seems he was a friend to Cats in particular, so much so that at times he is depicted with a Cat, as in a painting by Antonello da Messina (c. 1450).

Children who had lost their own four-footed friend would recite the little poem with fervor, certain that the good saint would hear them. Today the routine is different. If you lose a Cat (and how many are lost! though it's not clear whether this is due to a feline yearning for freedom or to distraction or insufficient concern on the part of their two-legged friends)... As we were saying, if you lose a Cat, you print his most recent photo on the computer, accompanied by the usual caption: "Lost" or "Lost, on such-and-such a date, male (or female), by the name of... Generous reward, etc.". You make a certain number of copies, and affix them to tree trunks, alongside front doors, and in the windows of the vet's offices. As if the Cat knew how to say his or her name in human-speak! It is rare that we find them, however. And we don't know how to react to the void they leave. Nevertheless, a song, published for the first time in 1893 in Anglo-Saxon countries, assures us:

But the cat came back the very next day,
The cat came back, they thought he was a goner.

But the cat came back, he just wouldn't stay away.

Over the course of time, the popular imagination has added (and continues to add) stanzas to this old song which are inspired by events having nothing to do with the world of cats but which have a certain relevance to human life and history. This was the case even for the dramatic explosion of the H bomb.

A song which Pussy Meow likes very much, perhaps because of the rhyme, perhaps because of the joy with which we sing it, is a little Italian song – yet another nursery rhyme for children – which is much more recent and was a prize winner in the "Zecchino d'oro", a TV competition for children. Its somewhat martial refrain goes like this:

> Forty-four cats in rows of six, with two left over were marching tightly in rows of six, with two left over.

Cocontemporary Italian singers have also written poignant songs about cats, such as Gino Paoli's "La Gatta" (The Cat) – which tells of a cat with a black spot on her muzzle who would purr whenever the singer slung his guitar on his shoulder – and "Maledetto di un gatto" (Damned Cat) written by another song writer-singer.

Songs about Cats have been published since the eighteenth century. For the most part, they are love songs, which can relate to both felines and humans. The majority of them are Anglo-Saxon. One of the oldest is the song of the Cats at midnight. It goes back to the last decade of the eighteenth century and compares the way Cats with Humans make love. Almost contemporary to it is the story set to music of the Wicked Old Woman. She was wicked because she left all of her possessions to her Cat, instead of to her grandchildren.

A long, poetic homage to His Majesty is cited in a bestseller from about twenty years ago, Tad Williams' "The Tailchaser's Song". The author of the poem is Christopher Smart:

"For I will consider my Cat... For at the first glance of the glory of God
in the East he worships in his way.

For this is done by wreathing his body seven times
round with elegant quickness.
For having done duty
and received blessing he begins to consider himself.
For this he performs in ten degrees".

The listing of the degrees is lengthy but delightful just the same:

"For first he looks upon his forepaws
to see if they are clean.
For secondly he kicks up behind
to clear away there.
For thirdly he works it upon stretch
with the forepaws extended.
For fourthly he sharpens his paws
by wood.
For fifthly he washes himself.
For sixthly he rolls
upon wash.
For seventhly he fleas himself,
that he may not be interrupted upon the beat.
For eighthly he rubs himself against a post.

For ninthly he looks up
for his instructions.
For tenthly he goes in quest of food.
For when his day's work is done,
his business more properly begins.
For he keeps the Lord's watch
in the night against the adversary.
For he counteracts the powers of darkness
by his electrical skin and glaring eyes.
For he counteracts the Devil, who is death,
by brisking about the life.
For in his morning orisons
he loves the sun and the sun loves him.
For he is of the tribe of Tiger.
For the Cherub Cat
is a term of the Angel Tiger.
For there is nothing sweeter
than his peace when at rest.
For there is nothing brisker than his life
when in motion.
For God has blessed him
in the variety of his movements.

For he can tread
to all the measures upon the music".[2]

The author of this long, poetic series of merits restores dignity to the Cat by virtue of his being God's creature. It calls to mind the initiative of a high-ranking prelate in Rome, once pastor of the Church dedicated to Saint John of the Florentines. The priest was a great friend of Cats and of all animals in general, recognizing and worshiping in them the hand of God. Accordingly, he instituted a Mass intended just for animals and their owners. He himself celebrated it, every Sunday at noon. We went there with a broadcast technician to tape what in journalistic jargon is called a "colorful news feature" and were surprised by the silence that attended that religious function. Of course, there was an unusually large, curious crowd. But there was no meowing, no barking, no peeping. Not even Humans are that quiet in church. We are also reminded of a compassionate episode, reported by newspapers at the time, which had to do with one of Pope Paul VI's many visits to the various parishes in Rome. The Pontiff became aware that one of the children pressing around him seemed sad, and asked him what was the matter. Through his tears, the boy replied that his little Cat had died that very morning. The Pope consoled him, assuring him that when he became very, very old and had concluded his life on earth, he would find his little Cat waiting for him in heaven.

We continue to wonder: "Does our beloved Cat know all these things? We should tell him about them. They would undoubtedly give him pleasure".

N.B. Of course I am aware of these things. Quite frankly, I could comment on the metrics and the ideas expressed in these rhyming compositions, but I'm feeling magnanimous. Not arrogant. So I'll pass. Signed: yours truly, Pussy Meow.

[2] Excerpted from Christopher Smart (1722-1771): "Jubilate Agno".

More music, master Cat

We've observed them listening to music. Yes, they love music but they don't like the "noise" which so excites young Humans at discotheques, for example. Yes, they appreciate the Beatles, just as they appreciate Bach. They purr not only while listening to the chords of a guitar, but also while listening to the sweeping rhythm of a Viennese waltz. On the other hand, we don't know what they think about compositions dedicated to them, since no one has yet asked them. Among the most celebrated is the one composed by Rossini, a duet as amusing as it is difficult, based on an exchange of "meows" between a male and female voice. No less famous are the 1921 jazz classic "Kitten on the Keys" by Zez Confrey, and well before that "La fuga del gatto" (The Fugue of the Cat), composed by the great Domenico Scarlatti. Like Confrey, the eighteenth century harpsichordist also imitated the

prancing of one or more quadrupeds on the keyboard. Equally renowned, needless to say, is Tschaikovsky's ballet "The Sleeping Beauty" with its feline presence. Moreover, the ballet actually pays tribute to catlike agility with one of its most difficult dances, which is in fact called the "pas de chat". But as usual not even music manages to steer clear of the barbarisms perpetrated upon these poor creatures, who are more than justified for having become somewhat anti-social toward Humans. We are alluding to the so-called "cat organs" which greatly amused a certain type of public between the sixteenth and eighteenth centuries. These were boxes in which the unfortunate victims were confined, leaving only their tail free so as to allow the... player of the "instrument" to pull it, provoking, let's say, the most intense expressions of protest. And to think that in our own day there are people who detest those feline displays which take place on rooftops or in courtyards as a way of proclaiming the pleasures of love, the hopes of a bunch of enamored suitors, and the disappointment of others. They call them excruciating choruses. What about the sounds produced by the above-mentioned "organs", what should they be called? Less barbaric, since flesh-and-blood-and-fur Cats are not involved, are several more or less exotic instruments which are nevertheless inspired by feline meowing. These include the Javanese saron, a kind of bell, made of bronze, which produces mewing sounds, and the samisen, a traditional, three-stringed Japanese instrument, similar to a guitar, used by strolling musicians both in tea houses and at geisha gatherings. A musical saw, played by varying the tension of the blade and striking it with a hammer or violin bow, can produce sounds which, if not actually harmonious, are at least not unpleasant. And then there is the sistrum, a percussion instrument composed of a frame on which rings and bells are hung, which in ancient Egypt was played in honor of Isis. By rattling the rings and bells, sounds similar to yowls are produced. In many depictions of the cat goddess Bastet, she holds a sistrum in her hand.

Harsh awareness

My Human had added yet another one of her many questions. It is:

Do our Cats remember all these things? Yes, almost certainly, because often we see traces of sad memories, joys and splendors passing across their mysterious gaze.

I have repeated both her question and her reply in the present commentaries because they are useful in allowing me to introduce a new topic. She agrees with those who maintain that we are indeed likable, intelligent, possessive, authoritarian animals, but also very, very mysterious. I take great pains to make her believe she is right as far as this last consideration is concerned, because it serves to pique her interest toward me. Thus, when I don't want to be disturbed, I exaggerate – how shall I put it? – the inconsistency of my behavior, so that she will stop whatever she's

doing and observe me attentively. Based on these... studies of hers, she has written in other books (see What Did The Cat Say? *and* How To Obey Your Cat) *that we Cats not only want to be the center of attention, but that we demand the respect of autonomy and independence. This is where our disagreement begins, since, according to her, our definition of independence is nothing more than freedom to do whatever we want. But Humans are not always willing to comply with certain demands on the part of His Majesty, she says, especially when he would like to walk along the eaves or on a fourth floor windowsill. So she advises acting shrewdly, convinced – sweet heaven! – that we do not understand certain subterfuges. I would like to remind her how dearly our freedom has cost us – and perhaps still costs us – and how merciless those Humans can be who want to force us to renounce it in order to be with them. According to popular belief, for example, the tip of a Cat's tail should be cut off – think how barbarous! – and buried under the doorstep in order to keep him at home and to stop him harboring any notions of flight. Less drastic is the version according to which it is enough to bury a few hairs from his tail. If you want to overdo it and be sure of the result, you can place the tuft between two little sticks.*

If only it were a matter of restricting our movements! The superstitiousness of the two-footed ones knows no bounds. At one time, in Anglo-Saxon countries, a white Cat would be walled up alive in one of the outside walls of a new house in order to assure prosperity – let's hope that certain customs have been shelved. In Latin countries, even today, black Cats are feared because it is said that they bring bad luck. This is why I advise my fellow cats with dark coats not to cross the street at night. And, if possible, not even during the day.

Shame on you, Humans! You should reflect on the thinking of a Dutch researcher who believes that there isn't one single quality of a Cat that man could not emulate to his own advantage. But do you Humans know how to reflect? I've never seen you sit on the page of a book and stare intently at a point in space. It's therefore useless to prod you, you Humans.

Let's tread carefully, then

We have reflected, dear Pussy Meow – not that we needed to – and we agree that we must really tread carefully with you. The reasons for this? We shall list them for you:

Touchiness. To begin with, it is a good idea to spare you any offensive epithets, even when you cook up one of your mischievous pranks. Not because we are afraid that you may respond in equally...vivid terms. Perhaps you will, but since we do not know cat language very well, we are not able to take offense. The fact is that you are one of the touchiest creatures around, and you always adopt the philosophy – as those who speak with refinement say – of giving tit for tat. We are familiar with your retaliations, all the more so since you do not lack creativity. "Choose, my dears", you must surely say to yourself, "do you want me to sharpen my claws on the sofa, or would you prefer that I go and rummage in the sewing basket, pulling out spools and balls of yarn which I will enjoy rolling under the furniture?". In addition, it is better not to say to you "You're an alley-cat", even when you make us lose our patience. We know you prefer to be described as a free Cat or as a mongrel Cat.

Jealousy. Your touchiness is often mistaken for jealousy. And the latter for surliness. In fact, the line between these emotions is not well defined in your nature. Needless to say, however, it is always we Blah-Blahs who are to blame for arousing one or the other of them. What do we do wrong?

1) Petting an alien Cat. It is useless to even do it behind your back. You always know, since all it takes is the other cat's scent – which you can smell on our hands – to get on your nerves;

2) Not cuddling you when you want to be cuddled and sidestepping you when you rub your back against our legs;

3) Leaving you alone in the house or garden for a very long time. Too long;

4) Informing you when we have to be away for a

while. It's not worth the bother: right away you begin acting like a troglodyte;

5) Showing affection or excessive concern for a friend. Or at least for someone who does not have a permanent place in the family circle, of which you consider yourself to be the tutelary deity;

6) Forcing you to accept a guest's presence for a little while, which will inevitably upset the order you have pre-established. And urging you to be polite. Are we crazy or something?

Spitefulness. As for the other emotions listed above, when something sticks in your craw, you have many ways of showing it. Even if it means risking punishment, obviously. "You don't want to let me out on the balcony with the excuse that you've just cleaned it? Then I, who feel an impelling need to sharpen my claws, will do so on the bottom of your ever-so-comfortable mattress". Or: "You don't want to refill my bowl? Okay then, I'll play billiards with the knickknacks on the parlor table".

There's no need for words. It's the thought that counts, one might say if he were feeling witty.

Respect his privacy

Master Cat willingly plays with his Human, especially when he doesn't have a companion of his own species. In that case, he designates the two-footed one with whom he lives to act as mama or brother. The games can become very amusing at times, if not violent. The imagination of a playful Cat can seem boundless. Pussy Meow, for example, is a champion at playing hide and seek. But he always wants to be the one to win. His fun, in fact, consists in devising ambushes to ensnare the legs of the Human who finds him hiding behind the door. Then, too, he has invented a kind of golf game which we could describe as cat-golf. All that's needed is a ball and a little stick to nudge the ball under the furniture. The Human plays the role of caddie, assigned to retrieve the ball by manoeuvering the stick, since Pussy Meow is not able to. He's tried to manoeuver it with

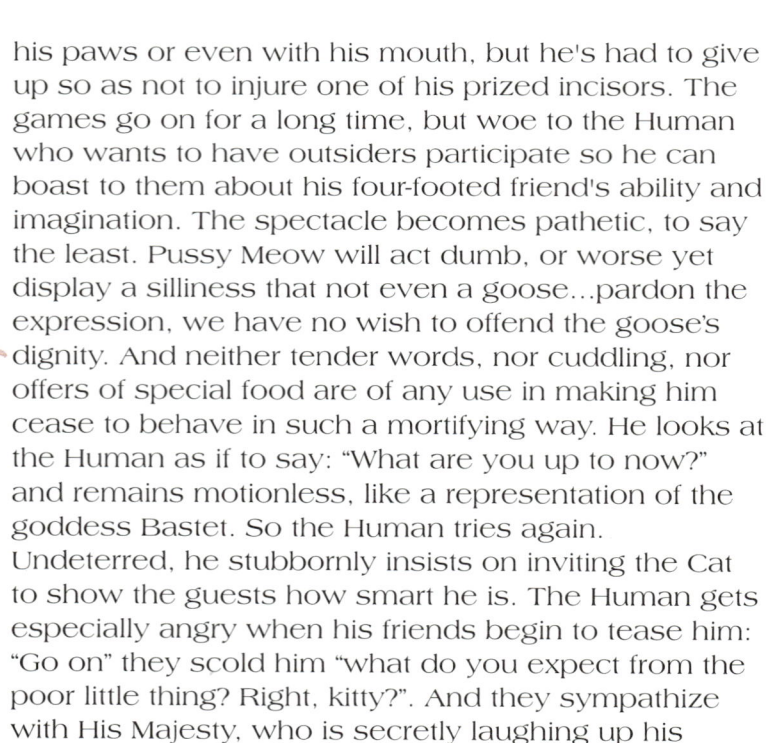

his paws or even with his mouth, but he's had to give up so as not to injure one of his prized incisors. The games go on for a long time, but woe to the Human who wants to have outsiders participate so he can boast to them about his four-footed friend's ability and imagination. The spectacle becomes pathetic, to say the least. Pussy Meow will act dumb, or worse yet display a silliness that not even a goose…pardon the expression, we have no wish to offend the goose's dignity. And neither tender words, nor cuddling, nor offers of special food are of any use in making him cease to behave in such a mortifying way. He looks at the Human as if to say: "What are you up to now?" and remains motionless, like a representation of the goddess Bastet. So the Human tries again. Undeterred, he stubbornly insists on inviting the Cat to show the guests how smart he is. The Human gets especially angry when his friends begin to tease him: "Go on" they scold him "what do you expect from the poor little thing? Right, kitty?". And they sympathize with His Majesty, who is secretly laughing up his sleeve, until his two-footed one resigns himself to the evidence before him. Then, as soon as the Cat sees that the coast is clear, he slinks away, so that he, at least, hasn't lost his dignity. It matters little to him that his Human has lost face. So much the worse for the arrogant fool who wants to show him off in front of people he doesn't know well; and who, above all, doesn't have the delicacy to respect the privacy of others. Even that of a Cat.

This is why the Cat has not often appeared in circuses, not since earliest times. He has a lot of self-respect, and doesn't like to be taken for any old buffoon. It must certainly be his genes which prompt him to be this way.

Human, respect our ancestors too

They were magnificent ancestors. Not only respected, but venerated, especially by peoples of the East, above all the Egyptians. The latter actually prohibited the exportation of us Cats because they valued us as custodians of their grain storehouses. Our presence kept the mice away. It was the Egyptians themselves who saw to our education, who more or less tamed us in order to make better use of our abilities. And they showed their recognition of our worth in a magnificent way by actually deifying us; there were more feline deities in their paradise than anthropomorphic gods. When did we make our first appearance in Egypt? If I remember correctly, it was following the conquest by Sesostri, the Ethiopian commander from Nubia. History is not my strong point, and to learn about it I endured a number of cuffs from my real mother, poor Cat, which I can still feel on my withers. She was a fount of knowledge, but I was most recalcitrant to her teaching efforts. However, I think I'm correct in saying that we migrated by following the Nubian army toward the Egyptian valleys, where we were received very, very warmly. And yet, it seems we were not at all as beautiful as we are now. At least according to old portrayals which depict us with either very short ears and a flat nose, or rather long ears and a pointed nose. Also much disputed is the color of our fur. As my Human would say, there are two schools of thought about that. According to one of them, our Egyptian forebears were gingerish, streaked with black; according to the other, our coat was dark gray. In any case, our hair was short, just like mine. So much for the Princess and the airs she's always putting on. So there!

We are taking possession of the keyboard again in order to pose a question to our encyclopedic co-author: by virtue of which gifted qualities did the

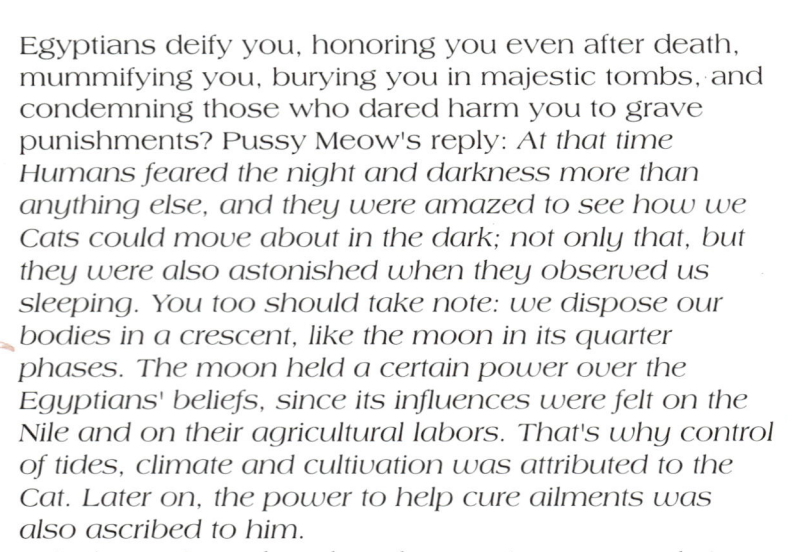

Egyptians deify you, honoring you even after death, mummifying you, burying you in majestic tombs, and condemning those who dared harm you to grave punishments? Pussy Meow's reply: *At that time Humans feared the night and darkness more than anything else, and they were amazed to see how we Cats could move about in the dark; not only that, but they were also astonished when they observed us sleeping. You too should take note: we dispose our bodies in a crescent, like the moon in its quarter phases. The moon held a certain power over the Egyptians' beliefs, since its influences were felt on the Nile and on their agricultural labors. That's why control of tides, climate and cultivation was attributed to the Cat. Later on, the power to help cure ailments was also ascribed to him.*

At times, Cats also played a very important role in Egyptian military history. Like the time, around 500 B.C., when the Persians and Egyptians faced each other in battle near the city of Pelusium. The Egyptians were beginning to gain the upper hand, when their enemies adopted a stratagem which turned the fortunes of war in their own favor. The Persians withdrew from the battlefield for a few days and, when they reappeared, every soldier held a cat in his arms; other Cats had been set loose and were running crazed and frightened among the legs of the warriors. Because the death of a feline was severely punishable in Egypt, and because of the danger of wounding one of them, the Egyptians dropped their weapons and were resoundingly defeated.

These are wonderful stories, in large part true, in fact, for which we take our hats off to you, Pussy Meow.

And should we mention his connections in Paradise as well?

Should we also mention his connections – let's say – to the residents of Paradise? After Saint Jerome, the only saint to be depicted with a Cat (see Poets and Bards for Sir and Lady Cat), many saints were associated with felines in the Medieval period, despite the persecutions to which the poor creatures were subjected as a result of gullible individuals who thought they were related to the devil. Persecutions fed by foolish, bloodthirsty superstitions. Some actually went so far as to believe that the Cat inhaled children's breath in order to suffocate them.

Saint Gertrude of Nivelles is recognized as the patron saint of Cats. Female Cats had a friend in Saint Agatha, also called Saint Cat as a result of a misunderstanding arising from the distortion of her

name.[3] Saint Ives, patron saint of lawyers, was sometimes depicted as a Cat, not because of his sympathies toward felines – on the contrary – but because the quadruped symbolized the negative qualities of some attorneys. This showed a real lack of gratitude toward the saint, given the fact that he was also known as a patron of the poor. However, once the nasty historical moment was over in which Pretty-Tails had quite a bad time, many artists surrendered to their grace and charm. We therefore find them appearing frequently in paintings, especially from the sixteenth century on, even in sacred representations, in fact. Earlier still, Pietro Lorenzetti had placed one in his "Last Supper", found in the basilica of Saint Francis of Assisi. The painting dates back to 1320, therefore to the late Middle Ages. Certainly the Cat does not have a commendable role in the painting: he is shown in an adjoining room competing with the dog for the leftovers. According to Suzanna Sebkova Thaller, the quarrel should be seen in relation to the curse of original sin inherent in Judas' betrayal, with both the dog and the cat representing evil. A peaceable, satisfied Cat appears instead in a painting of the Annunciation attributed to Tintoretto (c. 1570), found in Rotterdam. In the Church of Ara Coeli in Rome, a beautiful Cat is depicted alongside the Virgin in a painting by an anonymous artist, commonly referred to as the "Madonna of the Cat". While the feline presence is linked to negative symbolism in a great many representations of a sacred nature, we have only to look at periods closer to our own time in order to see Pretty-Tail's role restored to a normal order with no underlying preconceptions. For example Franco Gentilini's oil on canvas, "Cat with a Ball of Yarn" or Emmanuel Frèmiet's little bronze, "Kitten Washing Itself", for example, both from the last century.

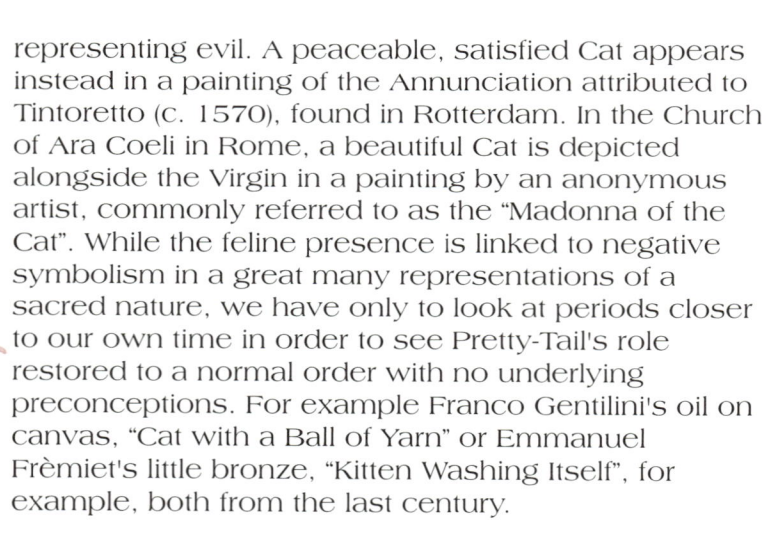

[3] Saint Agatha, Sant'Agata in Italian, might have been corrupted into Santa Gatta (Saint Cat).

Don't tell him, don't do it

Here is some advice which we think may be useful to Humans who are dealing with a Cat with a capital "C", that is, one with a sensitive temperament.

1) Don't try to dissuade His Majesty from concluding a noisy brawl with one of his neighbors during the siesta hour, even if the dispute, though merely verbal, risks causing a condominium uprising just the same. Nor should you try to make him give up his enthusiastic pursuit of a harmless gecko. It's useless to say to him: "Don't do it, that's enough, stop it";

2) Don't rub his nose in his urine if he's preferred using the carpet or even the bed of one of the Humans instead of using the litter box. A smack? Maybe, but the punishment must be timely; if it isn't, the guilty party might wonder why you are punishing him. At least that's what ethologists and vets tell us. Then again, maybe he knows very well why you're punishing him. Instead, we should ask ourselves why he behaved in such a reprehensible way;

3) Don't threaten him. It's sad to see a Cat slinking around timidly in the street, ready to jump out of reach of a human shoe. Such a creature must surely be used to threats. It's like seeing a beautiful work of art going to ruin. The Cat who is sure of himself and of being welcome, advances with his tail held straight up like a periscope. Shakespeare left us the memory of a harmless, necessary cat, not of a mortified little creature;

4) Do scold him when necessary. Despite his bravado, we consider Pretty-Tail to be rather sensitive to oral reproaches, even though he doesn't show it. At times "dirty little slob", works wonders.

His Majesty is not a dog, and he considers it important not only to draw the distinction, but to emphasize it by his own behavior, just in case the Human he lives with hasn't realized it. The dog – if we can guess the feline's thinking – obeys, albeit reluctantly. The Cat, on the other hand, is determined to remain his own boss, a tenacity which he displays over and over again.

A family memory, passed down to us from father to son, seems especially fitting here. In the peaceful, almost sleepy Rome of the first decade of the twentieth century, Alì, a black, medium-sized poodle, shared his existence in our family (animal lovers ante litteram) with hamsters, guinea-pigs and Cats. He was very proud of an assignment he had been given by the most important Human in the family, a task which he did each day. "Alì" she would say to him at twelve o'clock on the dot, "go and pick up the children at school". And the dog, aware of the importance of the mission, would set off at a run to position himself in front of the school entrance ready to gather up the children of the house. Even if one child had already handed over his school bag to him, if another lingered to play with a classmate, Alì would set the bag on the ground and chase after the disobedient child. The Human could never have entrusted one of the Cats with the task, not because he wouldn't have obeyed, but because he would have arrived unequivocally and irremediably late to meet the children, having been distracted along the way;

5) To put an end to a quarrel between felines or between a feline and a dog, should the situation become serious and the neighbors' protests unbearable, try to soothe your fuming quadruped by offering him a

good meal, or fool him with the sudden sound of the doorbell. Curious as he is, he will call a halt to diatribes, claims and entanglements to run and see who the visitor may be. The same ruses may be used to convince him to stop chasing geckos, blackbirds, sparrows, butterflies and other unwary little creatures. If they do not work, you can always resort to the thwack of a newspaper at a point closest to the where the cat is performing, or a squirt of water, provided the editors and typographers aren't on strike and the season isn't too cold to run the hose. The newspaper is an object for which Pretty-Tail has an incurable aversion. Even Cats who live with journalists feel this way. Perhaps because they view the newspaper as something which draws the Human's attention away from them; perhaps because dogs are so enthusiastic about carrying the papers between their teeth to bring them to their masters; or perhaps –in our opinion, this seems to be the most valid reason of all – because they make an unpleasant noise and, as we know, Cats detest any kind of noise. That's why many Cats, as soon as they can, tear the newspaper into shreds.

Speak gently to him

Raising a Cat is not easy, especially if you get him when he is no longer a kitten. The assumption is – and it does not seem to be an exaggeration – that both the Human and the Feline must adapt to one another. Is it more demanding to deal with a dog or a Cat. And why? The dog cannot do without his walk twice a day and must obviously be escorted by the Human, supplied with plastic bag and small shovel (too often forgotten, in defiance of town ordinances). But that's another subject. And the Cat? His Majesty also needs care and concern. To get him used to his litter box, it is not enough to urge him with fond little words, especially when he is very little; you must do as his real mother would do, that is, accompany him to the litter box and gently guide his little front paws to teach him to make room for... what he can no longer hold.

Speak gently to him, yes, even when he wants to sharpen his claws in the least suitable places, but see to either cutting his claws or getting him a little scratching post or other object that he can scrape to his heart's content – there's a multitude of them, of varying shapes and styles, in shops specializing in such items.

We are against indiscriminately giving animals to children as gifts. Giving a Cat or dog, hamster or budgie, as a gift means not only enjoying its company but also being responsible for its care and feeding. Attending to a creature is not always as easy as it may seem. While it is true that an animal's presence may have a valid educational effect on a child, the choice should take into account both the pet and the the intended owner. Then too, if the gift is to be a large animal, the entire family should be in agreement, otherwise the innocent creature risks winding up out in the street at the first disturbance, hitch, or mishap – call it what you will.

Speak tenderly to him: the tone of voice, in other words, should be engaging. We have found that coaxing with your voice is sufficient to calm down a Cat – more so than cuddling – even if he is very angry. Nevertheless, Angelo Lombardi, the well-known ethologist who words we have quoted more than once before, had this witty remark to make: "...embroidered coverlets, big kisses, 'sweetheart', 'my darling' at every turn, these are all things... I'm sure, that will not make him mourn too much his wild and healthy rooftop sprints, perhaps in chase of mice".

How can you tell them?

For sure I will not tell them. But I can't stand hearing them fight. Even when they're just discussing (they say they're debating), what need is there to raise their voices? It seems like they hate each other. I know it isn't true, though, because I live with them and I know how they feel. They should take an example from us Cats: we only raise our voices when necessary. Even when we're 'debating', we use loving tones!

When the Humans tell me I eat too much and want to ration my provisions, I certainly don't protest by using rude words. No, instead I try to persuade them sweetly to give me an additional portion.

When they devote themselves to us, pet us and provide for all our needs, we would like it – I feel authorized to speak for the entire category of us Cats – if they were truly motivated by an interest in the so-called animal world, that is, if all the trouble they go to over our beds and food bowls did not mean that they consider us a substitute for children they don't have, don't want or cannot have. In short, we would like it if their affection were as genuine as ours is.

She wrote: We've asked ourselves many times why he loves us... why not only Cats, but also dogs and horses, and even little birds we keep confined in a cage love us. Because we look after them, perhaps? And just for a little food we give them, think how much they give us in return! Think how much good our Cat's purring does to our hearts – the friendly nudges of his head, the way he curls up in our lap, the trust he shows us. At times we ask ourselves if we deserve it. We especially wonder about it when we ourselves are not able to help our little friends, whereas they are able to help both us and other animals, or at least try to do so. Luis Sepulveda also believes that this is so, and depicts it in his very moving "Story of a Little Sea Gull and the Cat Who Taught Her to Fly". A tribe of Cats, led by fat, black Zorba, don't know which way to turn in carrying out the difficult task entrusted to Zorba by a sea gull dying after being drenched in oil. They have no other course open to them but to ask a poet for help and advice. The task, as we know, was that of brooding and hatching an egg, then teaching the chick how to fly. Zorba speaks to the poet in the human tongue, and at first the poet cannot believe his ears, and he slaps himself in order to wake up from what he believes is a dream. He brings his hands to his head and covers his eyes, repeating `it's because I'm tired', `it's because I'm tired'... You remember how the book ends, don't you? Zorba continues looking at the little sea gull until he no longer knows if raindrops or tears are clouding his eyes – the yellow eyes of a big, fat, black cat, a good cat, a noble cat, a harbor cat.

Why didn't we tell him?

When the Pussy Meow who for many years now has been resting beneath a pine tree in the garden, began to fall ill and we realized that his illness was serious and that we could do nothing about it, we weren't capable of telling him how much we loved him nor how much we feared a tomorrow without his presence. We often think back to the last of a long list of vet miracle-workers whose names had been recommended to us, and the trip we took to see him with Puss curled up in his big basket. It was a winter afternoon, cold and windy. We had to park quite a distance from the vet's office, even though we had driven around for some time to try and find a parking space in a particularly crowded section of the city. When we got out and started walking, the large basket which had weighed a ton when fully loaded – that is, when Puss was in good health – seemed unusually light. We didn't know how to carry it to avoid the north wind raking through it and freezing the poor little creature. Normally he would protest when he didn't like a situation. That day he did not. We tried to step up our pace to get to the vet's office, thinking it would be sheltered and warm there. But the office was still closed, and we began anxiously asking the neighboring shopkeepers what the surgery hours were.

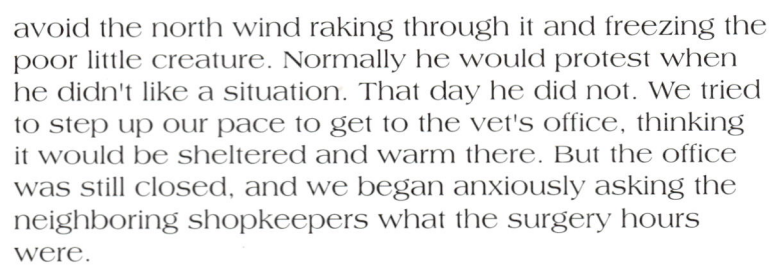

"Usually the doctor opens on time" they replied, adding "if he's not there yet, he must have had an emergency". We reproached ourselves for not having thought about the possibility of an emergency and for not having spared our poor Puss that difficult trip.

We didn't say to our four-footed friend: "You've been a good boy, dear friend, and we're ignorant fools. You're very brave, and if we made you suffer today, we only did it because we love you very much and we're trying not to lose you". Why didn't we tell him? Would he have understood us? We think he would have. After all, hadn't he understood – so many times – our physical, spiritual and mental discomforts and consoled us in his own special way?

A few words of encouragement

We end this labor of ours – not really labor but enjoyment – by acknowledging that a word of praise and encouragement is due to our Pussy Meow and to all his fellow Cats. The spoken word is a great gift of exchange which serves to re-establish an understanding, cement a friendship, and reinforce a bond of tender interest. Why not say it, then, to the friends who have been entrusted to us? Why not acknowledge that our non-human friends act as interpreters for us, and help us to understand not only every living being, but Nature as a whole, guiding us to recognize her in all her manifestazions, both positive and negative? Why not acknowledge that they act as substitutes for us, compensating – to our benefit – for our lack of that primordial instinct which we have lost as a result of so-called progress? Finally, since this handbook was written by two hands and two paws, we will let our co-author be the one to conclude it:

I hope our readers have appreciated my contributions; I have tried, in fact, to insert a word here and there among her annotations to keep them from crossing the line into pure fantasy. I am well aware of the notions she has about us. Nevertheless, believe me, I too have enjoyed this, even though I may have acted gruff. Because I'm not at all gruff, touchy, jealous, and so forth. The only thing I'm sorry I didn't get a chance to tell you about in more detail is that I finally managed to swat that puss over there, the Princess of my boots – if you catch my subtle irony. Another time, perhaps. Until then. Purringly Yours, Pussy Meow.

Table of contents

Introduction • 5

1. The controversial expedience of big words • 7
2. Don't tell the Human • 10
3. He must be given a name • 13
4. Names for them, the Humans • 18
5. Never let him know we suspect him • 21
6. Human culture: yuck! • 23
7. Lady Cats get it too • 27
8. What can we say about skinning the Cat? • 29
9. Annotations on the file • 31

10. A taboo topic par excellence: health • 35
11. Never say to him: let's go to the doctor • 39
12. You're on your own • 43
13. Ok, let's speak of health • 47
14. Top secret... It goes without saying • 50
15. Make him beautiful? Yes, but... • 57
16. Words are not superfluous • 64
17. Let's keep it a secret still • 68
18. Beauty contests: what a drag • 74
19. They don't need words • 78
20. For your own good, don't dare say certain things • 86
21. Feline enigma • 94
22. Poets and bards for sir and lady Cat • 97
23. More music, master Cat • 106

24. Harsh awareness • 109

25. Let's tread carefully, then • 112

26. Respect his privacy • 115

27. Human, respect our ancestors too • 118

28. And should we mention his connections In Paradise as well? • 122

29. Don't tell him, don't do It • 125

30. Speak gently to him • 129

31. How can you tell them? • 132

32. Why didn't we tell him? • 135

33. A few words of encouragement • 137

Don't forget two chapters amusing

GRAZIA VALCI

WHAT DID THE CAT SAY?

YOUR COMPLETE "CAT TALK" DICTIONARY AND PHRASEBOOK

120 pages • US$ 12.95

the other of this saga...

GRAZIA VALCI

HOW TO OBEY YOUR CAT

THE ULTIMATE HANDBOOK FOR THE SLAVISH CAT OWNER

120 pages • US$ 12.95